BOOK OF SCARY CREATURES IN THE PLANET

BABY PROFESSOR
EDUCATION KIDS

Parts of the world are filled with amazing, interesting and beautiful creatures. The rest of it is filled with terrible creatures that will haunt your dreams. We assembled a few list of the scariest, most terrifying creatures of earth.

GREAT WHITE SHARK

Great white shark is one of the most feared in the world, they are known for attacking humans. Of all shark species, the great white shark is responsible for by far the largest number of recorded shark attacks on humans. The great white shark has no natural predators other than the orca. It is arguably the world's largest known extant macropredatory fish, and is one of the primary predators of marine mammals.

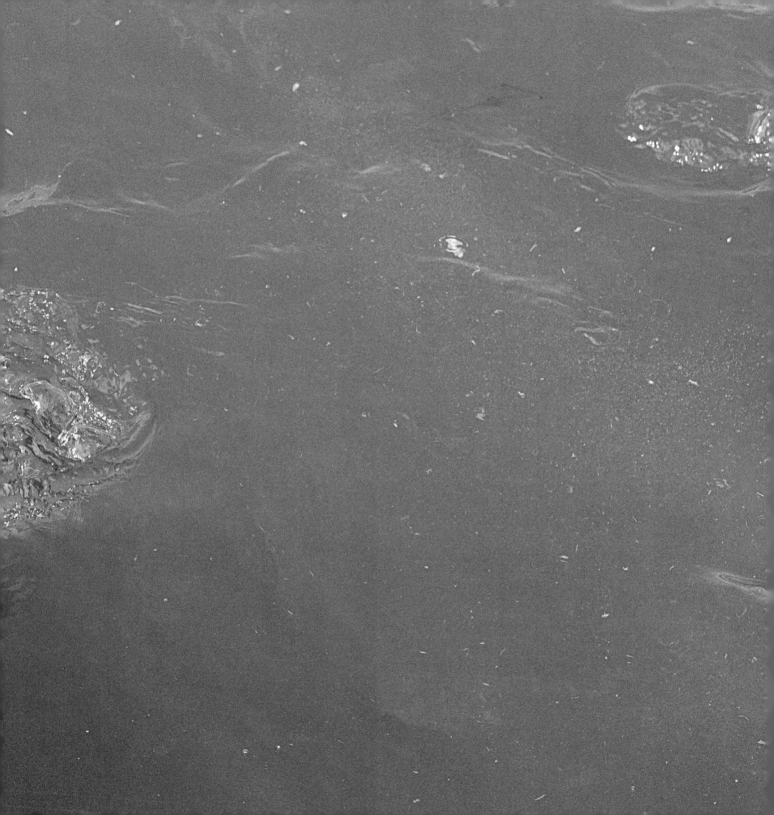

MOSQUITO

Mosquitoes are the deadliest animals on Earth. More deaths are associated with mosquitoes than any other animal on the planet. Thousands of species feed on the blood of various kinds of hosts. Mosquitoes can act as vectors for many disease-causing viruses and parasites. Infected mosquitoes carry these organisms from person to person without exhibiting symptoms themselves.

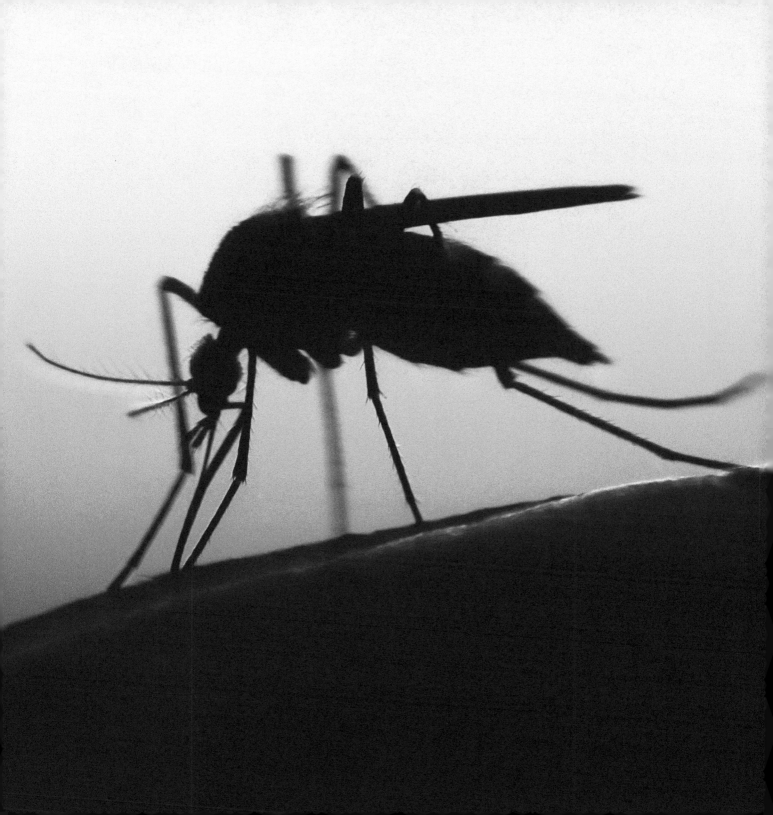

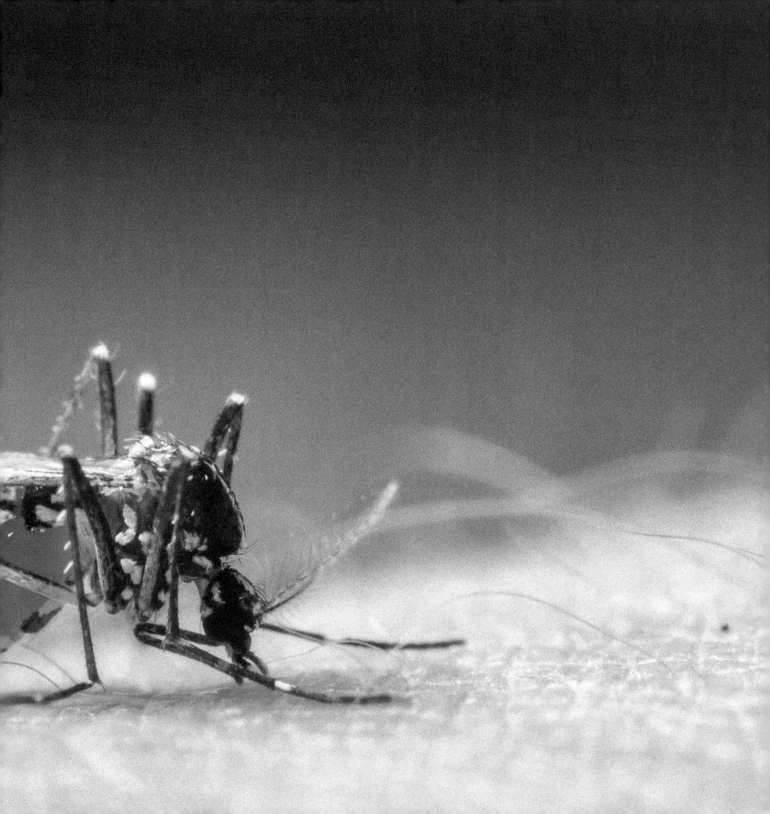

BROWN BEAR

Brown bear is a large bear distributed across much of northern Eurasia and North America and is the largest land-based predator on earth. Adult brown bears are powerful, top-of-the-food chain predators, but much of their diet consists of nuts, berries, fruit, leaves, and roots. Bears also eat other animals, from rodents to moose. They can be dangerous to humans, particularly if surprised or if a person gets between a mother bear and her cubs.

GILA MONSTER

Gila monster is a species of venomous lizard. Though the Gila monster is venomous, its sluggish nature means it represents little threat to humans. However, it has earned a fearsome reputation and is sometimes killed. The Gila monster lacks the musculature to forcibly inject the venom; instead, the venom is propelled from the gland to the tooth by chewing.

BLACK MAMBA

Black mamba is a highly venomous snake. It is the longest species of venomous snake in Africa, and the second-longest venomous snake in the world after the king cobra. The venom of the black mamba is highly toxic; potentially causing collapse in humans within 45 minutes, or less. The black mamba is capable of striking at considerable range and occasionally may deliver a series of bites in rapid succession.

KOMODO DRAGON

Komodo dragon is the largest living species of lizard, growing to a maximum length of 3 metres in rare cases and weighing up to approximately 70 kilograms. As a result of their size, these lizards dominate the ecosystems in which they live. Dragon saliva teems with over 50 strains of bacteria, and within 24 hours, the stricken creature usually dies of blood poisoning.

BOX JELLYFISH

Box jellyfish has been called the world's most venomous creature, containing toxins that attack the heart, nervous system, and skin cells. Human victims have been known to go into shock and drown or die of heart failure before even reaching shore. Once a tentacle of the box jellyfish adheres to skin, it pumps nematocysts with venom into the skin, causing the sting and agonizing pain.

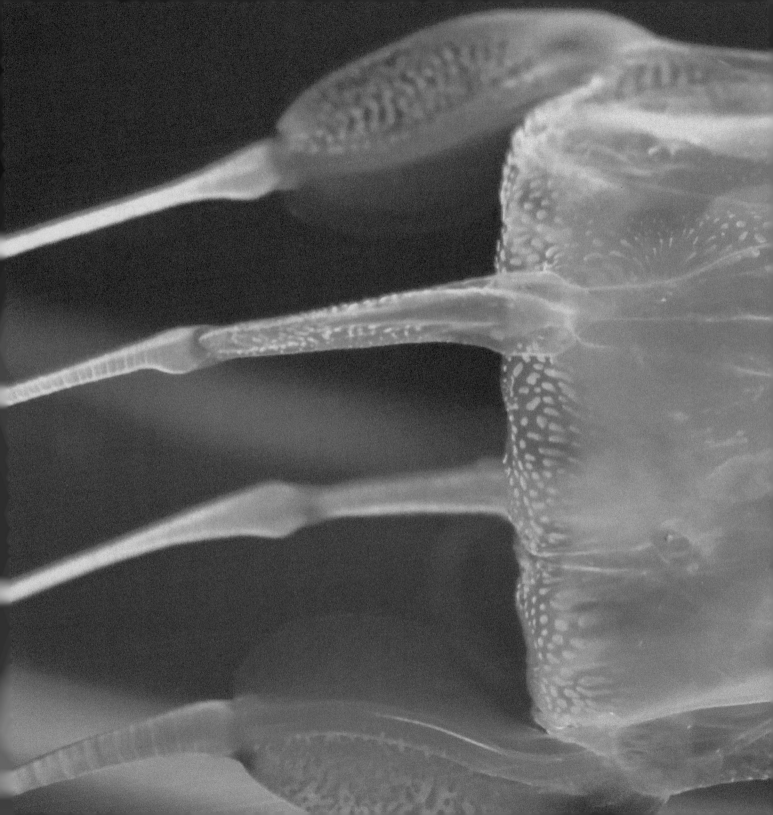

Lightning Source UK Ltd.
Milton Keynes UK
UKHW052046020123
414730UK00001B/1

9 781682 127742